Essential Electives for Homeschooling High School

How to Craft Courses That Exceed College Expectations

Lee Binz,
The HomeScholar

© 2019 by **The HomeScholar LLC**

All Rights Reserved. No part of this publication may be reproduced in any form or by any means, including scanning, photocopying, or otherwise without prior written permission of the copyright holder.

First Printing, 2019

Printed in the United States of America

Cover Design by Robin Montoya
Edited by Kimberly Charron

ISBN: 9781675897256

Disclaimer: Parents assume full responsibility for the education of their children in accordance with state law. College requirements vary, so make sure to check with the colleges about specific requirements for homeschoolers. We offer no guarantees, written or implied, that the use of our products and services will result in college admissions or scholarship awards.

Essential Electives for Homeschooling High School

How to Craft Courses That Exceed College Expectations

What are Coffee Break Books?

Essential Electives for Homeschooling High School is part of The HomeScholar's Coffee Break Book series.

Designed especially for parents who don't want to spend hours and hours reading a 400-page book on homeschooling high school, each book combines Lee's practical and friendly approach with detailed, but easy-to-digest information, perfect to read over a cup of coffee at your favorite coffee shop!

Never overwhelming, always accessible and manageable, each book in the series will give parents the tools they need to tackle the tasks of homeschooling high school, one warm sip at a time.

Everything about these Coffee Break Books is designed to connote simplicity, ease and comfort — from the size (fits in a purse), to the font and paragraph length (easy on the eyes), to the price (the same as a Starbucks Venti Triple Caramel Macchiato). Unlike a fancy coffee drink, however, these books are guilt-free pleasures you will want to enjoy again and again!

Table of Contents

What are Coffee Break Books? v
Exceed Expectations with Electives 9
The Basics of High School Electives 13
3 Ways Electives Make Homeschooling Better 19
3 Must-Have Types of High School Electives 23
3 Examples of Quirky High School Electives 31
The Sticky Note and Testing Strategies 45
How to Teach High School Electives 57
3 Situations That Make Electives Important 65
5 Steps to Create Records for Electives 71
9 Examples of Homeschool Electives 75
Finding Freedom with Homeschool Electives 85
Including Bible Classes on the Transcript 89
Who is Lee Binz and What Can She Do for Me?..93
Testimonials 95
Also From The HomeScholar 99

Introduction

Exceed Expectations with Electives

This book covers what electives are, which electives your homeschool should include, how to teach them, and which ones are most important. You'll also learn how to put these courses on your child's transcript. And we'll go in depth on frequently used elective courses so you can get some ideas and encouragement for electives in your own homeschool.

Electives are fun! They're called electives because they're largely your child's choice. And it's important for your teen to both enjoy their homeschool work and feel they have some control over it.

Electives are more important than you might think! When you make a solid plan for electives, you will have a roadmap to document how your teen will exceed college expectations. You will be able to paint a beautiful portrait of your student as a unique and qualified candidate. Electives will help your child shine on a transcript.

Your job is to educate your children, and colleges want to see rigorous college preparation in high school. By including electives, you can exceed expectations in many categories. Look at the college admission requirements for colleges your child is considering. Compare their requirements to the education you are providing your child. Is there anything missing? Can you exceed expectations with electives?

On your child's transcript, include all academic and natural learning, whether it was intentional or mandated by the state, or even worked on during the summer, when other subjects are on hiatus. Summer school counts, too!

Exceed expectations and put electives on your high school transcript!

Chapter 1

The Basics of High School Electives

Electives are often subjects your children do on their own instead of ones you assign. If your child is taking care of horses, you can call the class "Animal Husbandry." Designing draperies can be part of an interior design class. Let your teen decide on electives as much as possible.

There's no limit on the topics your children can study as homeschool classes. You can create fancy or plain class titles — whatever you prefer. And you can include delight directed learning (see Chapter 3 and 4) on your child's high school transcript as electives.

I'm sure that somewhere across the United States you will find brick-and-mortar public or private schools that offer the same elective classes you teach at home. Many high schools offer crazy-sounding electives that happen to be what the teachers are interested in. But in your homeschool, choices are not limited by what the teachers are interested in, only by what the child wants to learn independently.

What Are Electives?

Electives are like dessert. They are the non-core classes or credits that don't fit under the core categories. Every high school offers elective classes.

When I was in high school, one of my electives was a class called "Polynesian History." My teacher offered it so he could go to Hawaii every year and write it off as a business expense. My brother-in-law was a public school high school teacher and taught one elective called

"Sports Communication" and another elective called "The History of Baseball." He taught these two classes because he loved baseball and they allowed him to listen to games during class time.

In addition to electives that are required by homeschool law, you can choose electives that are important to you or fun for your student. Electives you want to cover aren't the same ones all homeschool families want to include. They don't even need to be the same for each of your children.

Sometimes the most valuable electives are life skill electives such as driver's education or keyboarding, logic, and computer skills — the kinds of skills adults use every day. Either adults have these skills or wish they did. You can make sure your student learns the skills you did not in high school.

And you can give your child personal time to pursue their passions. A little-known secret is that passion is an elective. When I was homeschooling, one of my boys loved chess and studied chess hours upon hours each year. One year we called those hours "Critical Thinking." The next year he began teaching chess classes and we called it "Public Speaking." The following year he got multiple chess jobs and worked for a chess company; we called those experiences "Occupational Education."

I know students who specialized in ornithology (the study of birds), mycology (the study of fungus), economics, and musicology. Specialization is one of the benefits of homeschool freedom. I encourage you to seize this opportunity so your child enjoys homeschooling even more.

How Many Electives?

On your transcript, add as many electives as your child earns. High school graduation requirements generally include 24 credits — English, math, social studies, and science, plus as many electives as it takes to earn 24 or more credits. When your child plays piano or guitar or basketball until late at night each day, it's okay to include these activities as electives each year they engage in them.

What Electives Can You Include?

Homeschoolers can tackle electives differently. You might want to include a crochet class, as I know so many homeschool girls who take crochet or knitting with them wherever they go. If your child does, that's great, include it on their transcript. School districts across the country include these kinds of classes and you can, too.

Wallingford Public School in Connecticut offers a class that includes crochet. They call it "Contemporary Crafts" and kids work on any yarn projects they want.

Northland Pines School District in Wisconsin offers a similar class called "Textiles, Arts and Crafts." Another school, Westwood School District in Michigan, includes a crochet class called "Creative Stitchery." Homeschoolers are simply doing what public schools already do. You can create your own classes and class titles.

Chapter 2

3 Ways Electives Make Homeschooling Better

1. Electives Make Teens Happier

One benefit of homeschooling is its efficiency, which allows plenty of time for fun. Electives make homeschooling fun. They mean less work for teenagers because electives don't require as many hours of formal schoolwork. Teens spend more hours on fun and less on directed schoolwork, so they often feel as if they're not doing schoolwork at all.

Homeschool parents know that all learning goes on the transcript, even if it's delight directed learning. Allow your teen time to engage in fun activities they love, while you follow behind and scoop up those credits.

Many activities teenagers do for fun can be used as high school courses. They make wonderful electives (and sometimes are additional foundation courses that beef up the transcript). This will help teenagers be happier when they're homeschooling, enjoy homeschooling more, and look back on it more fondly when they're grown.

2. Electives Make Parents Happier

Electives also make parents happier because there's less work when parents don't need to teach the class or find curriculum for it. Plus, there's less time spent grading and scheduling, and less money spent on curriculum. This makes parents happier because homeschooling is more enjoyable.

Electives should not always include a curriculum. Much of your schoolwork should *not* be curriculum-based and shouldn't be in a classroom setting. Many electives require little direction and you won't need to make them into a school class complete with curriculum.

Not only is the student engaging in more activities they consider fun and fewer things they consider work, parents are doing less work. It's not a lot of work to include electives — it's a matter of making sure your child has the time to devote to electives.

3. Electives Improve College Scholarship Opportunities

Colleges want to see unique interests and passions in potential students. Unique electives show that they are genuine interests and the child enjoys them. When a child enjoys an activity, they are more likely to develop a leadership position in that interest. It might start as an interest in technology when they start working on the soundboard at church. This can lead to a leadership position if they are eventually put in charge of the sound system at church.

It can also lead to perspectives that come out in each college application essay as they discuss their experiences. The result is not a cookie cutter kid — these kinds of electives lead to an activity and awards list full of genuine interests that colleges love to see.

Chapter 3

3 Must-Have Types of High School Electives

Every high school offers elective classes. What crazy electives were available at your high school? As I mentioned in Chapter 1, I took "Polynesian History" and my brother-in-law taught "Sports Communication" and "History of Baseball" at his public high school.

Homeschoolers are not limited by the whims of teachers or the preferences of principals or the school district. Instead, we can choose electives that are legally required, important to us, and fun for our students. These are the must-have electives to cover in high school, but individual electives aren't the same for all homeschool families, nor do they need to be the same for each child.

1. Electives Required by State Law

Each state has different homeschool laws. Usually the requirements involve subjects parents would teach their children anyway, such as reading, writing, math, science, and foreign language. That's why increased state regulation doesn't tend to affect homeschool performance. Truth be told, parents often have stiffer requirements than state laws.

However, look at your state law to see what is required, and find out if any of those requirements are electives. For example, Washington State requires that parents teach "Occupational Education." Other states might require "Technology" or "Computer Applications." Add these required classes to your high school class list.

Don't look up your state "graduation requirements." Those are requirements specifically for your local public high school, not for private schools or homeschools. Public school requirements change frequently, and may not reflect what is important or significant. Trying to meet public school requirements can lead to frustration and feelings of inadequacy. These requirements often stem from societal problems that are not meaningful in your homeschool. Look for electives required by your state homeschool law instead.

2. Electives Required by Parents

There are some subjects you believe should be required in high school, but aren't required by the state. That's one reason looking at public school requirements can be so frustrating – their inflexible guidelines can seem nonsensical in the context of your own child in your own home. Instead, look carefully at the subjects you believe are critical.

Subjects that parents require for high school vary significantly. One parent might require Bible classes while another requires auto mechanics or home economics. Your best friend might require logic, critical thinking, or debate. All homeschool parents choose different subjects they deem critical for high school. Add such subjects to your child's high school class list.

Set reasonable expectations for the number of high school classes your child takes. There are a million subjects you would love to teach your child, but you can't make your child learn in four years what has taken you a lifetime to learn. Each one credit class indicates about one hour of study per day for most of the school year. If your child takes more than eight classes each year, you are expecting them to sit still and study for more than eight hours a day. Is that reasonable? Keep your learning goals balanced, and don't expect your child to work longer than an adult works at a full time job.

3. Electives from Delight Directed Learning

Delight directed learning is also called specialization or child-led learning and colleges sometimes call it passion. It can be self-study, self-motivated, self-directed learning. These self-directed interests can develop into passions that lead to careers. The solution to dull drudgery and hated homeschooling is allowing it to happen naturally.

Learning for fun can take almost any form; it's not limited by the interests of the teacher, the school, or the purchase of a special curriculum. Any learning your child does for fun can be included on the high school transcript as electives.

To be quite honest, sometimes parents don't see these subjects as delight directed learning. Often, parents will see this learning as merely an annoying interruption. What is your child doing when they should be *doing school*? Could that behavior translate into high school credits? If they are constantly playing the banjo, riding horses, drawing anime, or mapping the moons of Jupiter, it can indicate some high school level learning.

Don't turn delight into a total drag. When your child is learning for fun, and you want to put that information on the transcript, the temptation is to force that subject into the public school mold. Don't do it! You don't want to beat the love of learning out of your child or make them hate their most-beloved pastime.

Don't make delight directed learning a boring school subject. You don't need to purchase textbooks (although your child may request some for further study). And you don't need to create tests. Instead, watch closely, listen, and learn from your children. They are capable of learning without any intervention. Your job isn't to make them learn, your job is to collect what they have already learned.

There can be impediments to learning for fun. If it seems like your child doesn't take joy in any delight directed learning, look for stumbling blocks that are getting in their way.

Sometimes the problem is simply a lack of maturity. Young students may need to explore more of the world before they *catch fire* for a subject. Sometimes the problem is time and a schedule crammed full to the gills. If they are so busy doing *school* each day, and don't have any free time, they may not have the necessary hours to learn how to enjoy other topics just for fun.

The problem might be technology if your child spends all their free hours glued to a screen, playing games or using social media. This kind of technology use can decrease creativity and enjoyment in other areas.

Delight directed learning requires time. Build margin into your homeschool and limit technology.

Chapter 4

3 Examples of Quirky High School Electives

Electives come in all shapes and sizes. I often get calls from Gold Care Club members who wonder if their student's passionate interest is a little too *off-the-wall* for colleges to appreciate. My answer is most often, "No, colleges will *love* it!" Colleges love teens who have gone beyond traditional education and found something that excites them.

In this chapter, I'm highlighting three of the *quirkier* electives I've seen turned into high school credits. In this case, *quirky* is not derogatory, it indicates the freedom to think broadly about what an acceptable elective is. If your child is passionate about one of these three subjects, that's great. You can make your child's homeschool records with confidence. If there's another oddball subject you'd like to chat with me about, consider joining my Gold Care Club (www.GoldCareClub.com) for a month or two!

1. Crochet

Mandi asks:

> My daughter has taught herself to crochet and makes bags, headbands, coasters, and whatever else pops into her head. Can we count it as an elective art credit?

Yes! Art can be taught intentionally through books or learned naturally for fun like Mandi's daughter is learning. School districts across the country include these kinds of classes. Let's look at a few examples.

A public school in Connecticut offers a class called "Contemporary Crafts."

Their online description suggests a variety of crafts. They call it "Career and Technical Education" instead of fine arts, but their students can earn a half credit each year. Here is their course description for inspiration to create your own:

Contemporary Crafts Course Description

Contemporary Crafts is a hands-on course designed to give students opportunities to develop skills in a variety of craft techniques. The course delves into the history of each craft and its application to today's society. There are numerous connections to the core academic areas. Each student will create an individual information based portfolio. The class will design a business based on a craft and market their product. Examples of the skills that may be developed include macramé, decoupage, charted designs, basketry, weaving, quilting, knitting, crocheting, paper craft, bookbinding, and stamping.

A high school in Wisconsin simply calls their course "Crafts 1." It's available every semester for students in grades 10 to 12, but you have the freedom to provide the same course in grade 9 if you wish. Their online description states:

> Some projects covered are: paper arts, cement casting, stamping, card making, clay, handmade books, fiber arts, and decorative painting.

Another school district in Wisconsin uses a fancy class title, "Textiles, Arts and Crafts." Here is their online description:

> Students will learn a number of handicrafts by taking this class. Students will work with the following areas in this class: crocheting, latch hooking, cross stitching, bracelet

making, scrap-booking, cake decorating, beading, and glass decorating.

A community school in Michigan calls their class "Creative Stitchery" for Grades 9 to 12. Although each semester class earns a half credit, the course can be taken more than once for credit throughout high school, so students can earn up to one credit per year. The school provides this description that you can also use for inspiration when creating your unique records.

> Creative Stitchery Course Description: This course explores hand sewing and craft techniques. The student will make a sample project supplied by the teacher. This allows the student to learn a hand craft such as knitting, crocheting, counted cross stitch, and/or embroidery. Students will be required to purchase some additional materials. As the student's

ability increases, each project will become more challenging. Because this class is taught according to each individual student's skill level, this course may be repeated to increase skill level.

You are not limited to these topics and can choose any number of skills to include in your homeschool class. Choose a fancy or plain class title, whichever you prefer.

2. Cosmetology

If your child loves to spend time painting nails or trying out all the hairstyles on Pinterest, why not consider cosmetology for a high school elective credit?

You can call this elective class "Occupational Education: Cosmetology." Some public high schools offer classes such as this and you can, too!

Consider putting together unit studies

for your child's areas of interest. You could include units such as massage, hair care, nail art, and makeup. Pick up books on each subject at your local library or look up the information online. No textbook is needed. Simply count the hours spent on everything cosmetology to determine the credit and include it on your homemade transcript. Once your child has spent about 120 to 180 hours of beauty school style training, you can call it a credit.

While you don't have to restrict yourself to the classes public schools offer, they can give you some ideas. Google "cosmetology education in high school" for examples of courses that are currently being taught.

3. Cosplay

For non-geeks, let me explain first that cosplay is a blend of two words, costume and play. It involves dressing up as a fictional character. Most often these characters are from a manga, anime, or comic book but they can also be from a movie or video game.

Let me translate this activity into high school credits for homeschool cosplay geeks. If your child is creating costumes, you can include this activity on their high school transcript. Make sure your child is sewing them on their own, with minimal help from a parent, much like they would in a high school arts class.

For the transcript, a good class title might be "Costume Design and Construction." Remember, a credit means your child worked 120 to 180 hours, or about an hour a day (4 to 5 hours a week) throughout the school year.

A grade of 4.0 means they successfully met your expectations with the work load and ultimately created the number of costumes you believe are representative of 120 to 180 hours of work.

Grading criteria option:

- 1/3 Design Work
- 1/3 Project Construction
- 1/3 Costume Presentation

Or more simply:

- 1/3 Daily Work
- 1/3 Sewing Labs
- 1/3 Final Project

Try choosing some of the words below for your cosplay class course description.

- analyze fibers
- analyze textiles
- basic costume construction
- character analysis
- consider design elements of

balance, line, pattern, shape, space, texture

- cosplay production
- costume design
- culminating project
- design
- design accessories
- drafting
- draping
- drawing
- evaluate fit on various body types
- evaluate garment construction
- evaluate cut and style
- figure drawing
- garment revision
- idea sample

- idea sketch
- initial design
- maintenance of apparel
- period research
- pre-project inspiration
- psychology of clothing
- rendering ideas
- research
- research popular styles and trends
- script analysis
- sewing
- textile characteristics
- utilize technology
- various textures

If your child is taking it to the next level by selling costumes or considering a future in costume design, your course description might include these words:

- develop a business plan
- develop marketing strategies
- explore career options in apparel
- explore careers in textiles
- marketing and sales of apparel

You can also list the tools used - fancy serger or embroidery machine, or basic sewing machine.

Combine the above words into sentences. Combine sentences into a paragraph. Voila! There's your course description!

Inspiration

I hope this chapter has inspired you to consider the unlimited options for electives and how they can be a great way to include more high school credits on your child's transcript.

With delight directed learning, it can be even more important to create a course description to include with your transcript. Somewhere across the United States, you can be sure another brick and mortar school is also offering the same kind of class. You can use public school course outlines to help you put together course descriptions. I offer a free training class on course descriptions you can take to learn more about how to do so, "Homeschool Records That Open Doors" at HomeHighSchoolHelp.com/homeschool-records-that-open-doors.

Chapter 5

The Sticky Note and Testing Strategies

If your child learns because they like it, don't teach it until they hate it. Delight directed learning occurs when a student pursues learning because they take great delight in the topic, not because it's a required course.

My son, Alex, was a self-motivated extreme learner. If only it were an Olympic event, like extreme sports! He learned novel writing for fun and wanted to take a third year of French even though I didn't have a curriculum for him. He asked for an "American Government" curriculum for Christmas and read every economics book he could get his hands on. Although his love language is reading, he was still a delight directed learner. When it was time to make his transcript, I still had to figure out how to translate his experiences onto a piece of paper.

For our family, the problem seemed huge. What should I do with all the experiences that cover a wide range of subjects? Was that report on Jean-Baptiste Say (the French Economist) a paper on history, economics, or foreign language? Was my son, Kevin's enjoyment of Russian history part of "World History," or could it be a course by itself? My children wrote *so* many papers that I didn't know what subject I should attribute them to! Where should I file each of them?

I found a system to help me sort out all their delight directed learning using my understanding of traditional grades and credits. It's easy once you get the hang of it. Once you understand how to calculate grades and credits using a textbook curriculum, it's easier to understand how to do it for delight directed learning.

The Sticky Note Strategy

What if your child soaks up knowledge like a sponge, without being directed? Some students learn best through living instead of studying textbooks. Can you still create a serious-looking high school transcript? Yes! However, nobody will ever know the fun or magical things your child has done unless you tell them.

When speaking to colleges, you need to use words and numbers they understand. Applying to college isn't like talking to your friend or a seasoned homeschool parent who understands the daily grind of homeschooling high school. Colleges understand grades, high school credits, and educational language. You need to keep those records.

Once I figured out how to keep track of

my kids' delight directed learning, I realized that my system would work for all delight directed learners (not only *book learners*). I also realized it could help parents who are kinesthetic learners. My strategy is simple, fun, and only requires one small purchase. Sticky notes. Those small square notes save the day again! You can determine what to do with each experience using a simple sticky note.

For each activity, there are five pieces of information you need to remember. Write these five things on the sticky note and save it with your homeschool records. At the end of each year, group those sticky notes together, and combine them to create high school courses.

I recognize it's hard to determine where each experience will fall on a transcript, so keep each sticky note simple. On each note, show the following details.

1. Name the Experience

On the middle of a sticky note, write the name of the experience. What did the child do? "Perform in The Nutcracker" or "crazy amounts of crochet and crafting." Write down any course title ideas, such as "Dance - Performance" or "Creative Crafts."

2. Note the Year

When did your child do this activity? Sometimes it will be a school year, such as 2019-2020, or it will be for a short duration, such as a play in November of 2021. Write this information in the upper left of the sticky note.

3. Grade the Experience

Did your student complete the project to your expectations? Were they successful, did they receive positive feedback, or learn something? You don't have to test to give a grade. Instead, you can evaluate in other ways. It's appropriate to give a Grade of *A* or 4.0 if your child has mastered the concepts, has high test scores, meets high expectations, or loves the subject and works excessively on it. Include this information in the upper right corner of the sticky note.

4. Note Credits Earned or Hours Spent

Count or estimate the number of hours your child spends on the project. A total of 75 to 90 hours is a half credit. If your child accumulates over 180 hours, it is a full credit. Or you might divide up the experiences into smaller, bite-sized pieces and regroup them into other courses with 180 hours apiece. If your child accumulates less than 75 hours, group the sticky notes together.

Keep sticky notes even when the activity required few hours. You can use experiences no matter how few hours your child spent. Note the number of hours and/or the number of credits earned in the lower left corner of the sticky note.

5. Consider Subject Areas

You may not know which subjects you will use for each experience, but record the possibilities. For our reports and papers, I often wrote several ideas on each note. One essay could be English, history, economics, or French. By making a note of it, I could decide later which course needed that experience to create a full credit. If history was already packed, I used another subject area. Write possible subject areas in the lower right corner of the sticky note.

Arrange into Affinity Groups

Once you complete sticky notes, don't review them until you begin working on the transcript. Checking too often can cause frustration and insecurity, so only review them when you start or update the transcript. This will help you keep the big picture in mind. When you are ready to work on your child's transcript, spread all the sticky notes on the table or floor. Then put them into "affinity groups" (groups of similar things). Work to combine sticky notes into groups that add up to one credit or half credit subjects.

Once you decide what goes into a course, include the course on the transcript. Make a note of the experiences you included on the transcript, if you want to. This will help when making course descriptions. Although you can change it if you need to, once you've decided on a credit, try not to stress about it again. Sorting your child's experiences into groups is a success. You have successfully grouped your child's delight directed learning into high school level courses!

This process of spreading notes out on the floor to group and regroup experiences is a great technique for any parent who is a kinesthetic learner. Even if you don't use a hands-on curriculum, this hands-on transcript process can help kinesthetic parents understand the nuances of their child's transcript. The process can help you remember what was included in each course — and even help write course descriptions!

The Testing Strategy

Another way to quantify delight directed learning is to give subject tests. This doesn't work for every subject or every child, but it's an option to consider.

Instead of testing your child as they are learning, allow them to learn a subject naturally. When they are done, give them a sample subject test from a major test provider. If they pass the sample subject test at home or at the testing center, you know how much they have learned and have a grade to put on their transcript. There are three tests available that will help with this strategy: SAT Subject Tests, Advanced

Placement (AP) exams, and CLEP tests from the College Level Exam Program.

Parents don't always know everything their children are learning. There is so much life that goes on without parental involvement — and so many books! It's amazing what children learn when you aren't looking!

Using CLEP exams, I found out how true this could be! I told my students to look over the exams "to see what they were like." One son passed an exam in "Business Law" even though I had never seen a law book in my home. He passed the "Principles of Marketing" test, even though I had never seen a marketing book in my home. He passed both "Micro and Macroeconomics," even though I'm still not sure what those two words mean. By testing my children, I could include some courses on the transcript that were a surprise even to me!

When using tests to document delight directed learning, be sure to avoid failure. Purchase a book with sample tests in it and give the exam at home first. Only take your student to an official test if you are sure they can pass. Your goal is to find out what they have learned, not to demonstrate what they don't know.

Find Balance

To homeschool high school effectively, include as much delight directed learning as possible. A fun learning environment does not make school easy, it makes it interesting and applicable. When school is interesting, children learn more and love learning more.

Parents need to find a balance, however. College preparation means parents must cover the core classes and at the same time allow for delight directed learning. When you can, cover the core and delight with independent learning.

When planning your week, first be sure to cover the core classes of reading, writing, math, science, and social studies. Each family has classes they consider non-negotiable core classes. When teaching these core classes, try to make them interesting. It's possible to teach many core subjects with delight directed classes, but be sure to cover the core.

Once you cover the core, capture your child's delights. Translate them into courses on your child's transcript. You don't have to plan, direct, or evaluate learning through tests or quizzes. Simply capture your child's learning.

Chapter 6

How to Teach High School Electives

You don't need a curriculum, quizzes, or tests to include electives on the transcript. Many electives are covered through natural learning that doesn't resemble school. Even without making these classes part of school, and even if they're working on it alone, you can still include quality learning on the high school transcript.

I encourage parents to educate with liberty — embrace your homeschool freedom and go classroom free. When you avoid the classroom mentality and avoid grade-level thinking, that's when you're educating with liberty. Your children will never be below grade-level again, and you'll recognize that learning is the key and not standardized tests.

With freedom to educate meaningfully, you can choose what fits your child's learning style and interests. Interested and engaged children learn more and learn better. The freedom to engage in unusual learning opportunities can help your child develop their passions, which will help them become better employees and choose their major.

Provide Time for Delight Directed Learning

Provide time for fun. Pursue a relaxed, fun, and educational experience. Yes, your child does need to get the hard stuff done first, including English, math, social studies, science, and foreign language in the morning, allowing time for fun all afternoon. The safe, secure, fun, and free environment of learning at home is a better way to educate children of all ages, even teenagers.

It's less stressful and takes less time so you want to encourage this delight directed learning. Again, you may need to cover those core subjects first, but the rest of this delight directed learning time can be fun. You need not make it into school; it can be unscripted and undirected.

Summer School or Christmas School

Consider when you usually take a break, such as in the summer or over Christmas holidays. During these times, you can relax, avoid teaching, and let your child learn naturally when you're not directing school. They can learn naturally, and you can include their delight directed learning on the transcript.

Your child can read books for pleasure. Encourage reading during the summer and during Christmas time; you can put aside a special, enjoyable book for your child to read. Pop in a DVD or stream a class; instead of directing Christmas school, they'll take in a Great Courses class over the holidays. Ensure your child reads books for pleasure and ask yourself whether it could be an elective when your child reads a lot on a specific topic.

During summer or *Christmas school* over the holidays, you can allow them to retain their skills as they do any test preparation. It isn't as much delight directed learning as it is you telling them what to do, but test preparation is a great elective they can take and handle on their own during the holidays. It goes on the transcript as study skills but it's not something you need to actively teach them.

Activities and Fun

There are so many fun activities your child could be involved in. For instance, sports (individual or team), music (taking lessons or learning through YouTube videos), or art. Church and other groups your child is involved with are often merely considered fun, but you might be able to include them on the transcript.

If your child belongs to the Bible quiz team or church youth group, these activities can become part of your Bible class. Speech and debate or civil air patrol can be on the transcript as well.

Classes Outside the Home

I rarely recommend forcing your child to take elective classes outside the home, but sometimes it makes sense, especially if you're not interested in teaching the topic yourself. Including a fluff and fun co-op class, such as a science class through cooking, makes a great elective. These co-op classes (or any subject beyond core classes they take outside the home), qualify as electives. For example, my child taught chess to homeschoolers. Everyone in his class could include "Critical Thinking and Chess" as an elective class.

Technology Classes

The biggest impediment to teaching high school electives is technology. It is tempting to think that all use of technology is an elective, but it's not. Sometimes technology is simply wasting time on the smartphone or computer. One of the best ways to include delight directed learning is to limit technology.

Kids need to be a bit bored to develop interests. When they're constantly on their phone, they never get that motivation from within to try something they find interesting. Technology can inhibit learning.

Technology is rarely used for high school credits. I usually see technology use causing less time for electives. Technology dependence prevents boredom, and boredom can lead to the development of genuine interests.

You can include some technology classes on your child's high school transcript. You cannot include social media or gaming. However, technology classes may include keyboarding, especially if your child is working on keyboarding skills.

Technology classes can include coding languages, or basic computer literacy. Include any classes on digital skills such as working online or with computers. For example, one girl I was working with wrote on her own blog daily. This was a genius move by her parents because that was the only way she was willing to write. She also included photography on her blog, so she was spending two hours a day blogging and earning one photography credit and one English credit.

A reasonable amount of technology use is about two hours per day, including schoolwork, social media, and gaming. This allows the teen enough time for fun but doesn't impede development of their interests. If you need help setting technology boundaries for healthy and happy children and teens, check out my book, *TechnoLogic: How to Set Logical Technology Boundaries and Stop the Zombie Apocalypse*, available on Amazon.

Chapter 7

3 Situations That Make Electives Important

Electives are great for all homeschoolers, but there are three situations that make them critical.

1. Electives for Gifted Learners

Electives can help gifted learners stay challenged so they continue moving forward and don't get bored. One way to find electives for gifted learners is to find a mentor — somebody who can understand what they're talking about and give them what they need to move to the next level. When my son, Kevin, played chess, we could not keep up with him. We were fortunate to find a chess mentor who ultimately hired my son as a chess coach.

Electives are great for gifted learners because they can lead to letters of recommendation that can help them earn scholarships and get into special programs. They can also give your child career options to consider. Will they like working at a think tank or writing books for publication? As they go through electives, your child is deciding whether they enjoy the subject enough to pursue it as a career.

For example, if your child doesn't want to work on homeschool at all and prefers mowing the local driving range, that makes a great "Occupational Education" class. It can help them with career discovery because they may decide that no matter what they do as an adult, it must let them be outside all the time. Or they may decide they don't want to be outside and prefer a desk job.

2. Electives for Struggling Learners

Primarily, electives can show students where they excel. Struggling learners often face what they struggle with all the time and can start to feel as if they're not smart. By providing electives, you can show them what they excel at and give them a boost of confidence. It wasn't until one of my friends' sons started working as a barista at Starbucks, that he started thinking he was smart regardless of his dyslexia, and was able to be successful.

Electives are terrific for career discovery and can be a source of letters of recommendation for struggling learners. For example, that same barista realized he didn't have to pour coffee as a career for the rest of his life. The letter of recommendation from his boss convinced him that he was smart enough to succeed at anything he wanted to pursue, so he decided to go to college for a business degree.

3. Electives for Special Needs Students

Electives are also great for those who need major help with school, either tutorial help or remedial help. They might need help with study skills or be on the spectrum and need to build social skills; they might be blind or deaf and need life skills or adaptive equipment.

Researching with one of my Gold Care Club members, I found out that one of the public schools in North Carolina puts social skills, life skills, and adaptive equipment on the transcript. The class title was general and didn't label the child at all — it was called "Curriculum Assistance." This is what they use for general school accommodation, including help with reading, writing, or processing issues.

There is also an independent study class that offers accommodations such as occupational therapy, physical therapy, and independent living skills. Southeast Riley High School puts special education services on the high school transcript when the student spends most of their day in the general education classroom.

If your child is learning braille, working with a seeing-eye dog, or getting help to walk independently, you can include all these skills on the transcript. Thinking about the ways these are helpful to kids will free up your mind to put them on the transcript. In public high schools, everything goes on the transcript, so you can include everything on the transcript as well.

Exceed Expectations

Your normal homeschool can be as impressive as any public or private school if you do two simple things. Number one is to make sure you cover the core classes because you always want to meet admission requirements. And number two is to capture delight directed learning with electives. That's how your child can exceed admission requirements.

Your job is to educate your child. Colleges want to see rigorous preparation, and by including electives you're delivering. Your child can exceed expectations in many categories. Admission representatives will look at how many classes your child has taken and may not notice one or two areas they might expect to see, but will definitely see what is *not* included.

Chapter 8

5 Steps to Create Records for Electives

How do you create records without a formal curriculum or a classroom setting?

1. Create a Class Title

Use the Sticky Note Strategy (see Chapter 5). For each of these experiences, create one sticky note. On that sticky note, you might write Tae Kwon Do, farm management, or small business or entrepreneurship. Writing down class titles can be helpful.

As you collect all these sticky notes with different class title options, group them together in affinity groups (similar topics), so you can create one class title covering a variety of similar experiences into one class. If your special needs child has engaged in occupational education, physical education, job training, or social skills training, these experiences could be gathered into one class called "Curriculum Assistance."

2. Calculate Grades

This is important to remember: you don't need to use tests. Consider how piano teachers evaluate classes. Most evaluate through watching and listening, not through fill-in-the-bubble tests. Observe and listen for your child's skills.

If your child meets your expectations, give them a grade of *A* if they love the subject and are doing well. If it is delight directed learning, chances are that they are doing well. If the subject is something you're making them do, they don't love it (and it shows), then you may need to give them less than an *A*.

3. Determine Credit Value

Scoop up the results of their electives like using a snow shovel after a winter storm. Consider what your child has accomplished and count or estimate the number of hours they spent.

You may wonder how you can ignore what they do and simply estimate hours. Often, your child is spending so much time on their passion that you only need to consider whether they are spending an hour a day or more on it. If they are, award one credit. For example, one of my children played the piano and I had to count his hours to determine if it was adding up to a whole credit.

My other child played the piano all day, even on weekends; I didn't need to count or estimate his hours since he was playing the piano for at least three hours a day, so I simply gave him one credit in piano per year.

4. Add to the Transcript

Include electives on the transcript. And don't forget to add the word "official" at the top of your child's high school transcript.

5. Write Course Descriptions

For every class, create a course description. Whether it's delight directed learning or not, you want to write course descriptions. Electives are as important as core classes, so write course descriptions for delight directed learning as well.

Some colleges want to see course descriptions for only core classes, while others want to see course descriptions for delight directed learning and courses they don't see every day. You don't know when course descriptions will be required. I recommend writing course descriptions for every class.

Chapter 9

9 Examples of Homeschool Electives

Your child doesn't need all the electives listed here; they are not required courses. These are simply some of the most common electives.

1. Occupational Education

I am so thankful that Washington State requires this elective because I learned so much about occupational education through the process of homeschooling. Even if you don't live in Washington and it's not required, you can still include it on your transcript.

Here's the sneaky way to include an occupational education course. Wait until your child is motivated by money and allow them to get a job. Count the number of hours they spend on the job, which can be easy because they get paid by the hour. Award a credit when they've worked 150 hours or more. You can go back when the job is done at the end of the school year and write a course description.

Your course description for occupational education should not only include the skills your child learned on the job. If they worked as a barista, for instance, they learned how to make coffee but they also learned general employability skills such as punctuality, handling their money, and opening a bank account.

2. Worship Team or Band

What do you do when your child is involved in worship team or band? You can include church worship band as high school credit and simply call it "Band." Keep in mind that if they lead worship as part of the worship team, this demonstrates leadership. If admission staff ask you what leadership positions they hold, being a worship leader is a leadership position.

You could also call band a fine arts class instead of an elective. Then your child is exceeding expectations in the fine art category. You can call it "Band with Performance" and write:

> In this course, the student will perform in a Christian church youth group band. The band provides an academic opportunity to participate in instrumental ensemble play. Special attention will be given to proper band routine habits, tone, production, intonation, skills, interpretation, and participation. Students are able to study and appreciate representative music of accepted value within the technical and intellectual range of their ability.

Then continue to describe in detail what your child accomplished.

3. Home Economics and Culinary Arts

Home economics or culinary arts classes can be as simple as your child making dinner every week. Some families are far more consistent than I ever was, and their children spend time planning a meal, developing the menu, shopping, baking, and cleaning the kitchen — for them, this is a huge culinary art class.

If your child is doing general work at home such as cooking, cleaning, and laundry, put it altogether into a home economics class. They're learning the skills of running a household.

For a culinary arts class, one of my Gold Care Club members listed all the menu items her child could cook. Another member's child worked on home economics; her course description included information about each skill her child learned through baking, sewing, cleaning, and budgeting.

4. Study Skills

Study skills are important for test preparation for SAT Subject Tests, the ACT, or CLEP tests. Anything for test preparation you can combine into one class called "Study Skills." This class can help your child prepare for college success. It becomes a catch-all class for interview practice or working on a resume — and can be part of a study skills, college readiness, or career readiness skills class.

5. Driver's Education

I recommend including driver's education on your child's transcript. Some colleges look at driver's education as proof homeschoolers are socialized and had a normal childhood. They want to know whether the child is independent enough to drive.

Driver's education may not be included on every local high school's transcript, but it is on many across the nation. Generally, schools give one half credit for driver's education. I put *pass* as my kids' grades and I think that was a mistake, so I encourage you to include a grade for your child's driver's education class. A grade of *A* once they pass the exam and get their license makes sense.

6. Logic

Another example is critical thinking (or logic). This is commonly a parental requirement. One of my children was into logic so we studied formal logic and bought a curriculum for it. Logic became one of our family requirements.

My other child loved critical thinking and chess because he was into logic. It's one of the reasons it was easy to see he was built to be an engineer when it came time to apply to colleges. He had both critical thinking and formal logic on his transcript as electives.

7. Scouting and 4-H

Through Scouts and 4-H, students gain many unique experiences that you can combine into classes. If your child is involved in scouting, they'll earn a P.E. credit every year, especially if they're an Eagle Scout. Or you can call it "Outdoor Education" instead. Scouting can involve skills beyond P.E. If they go to extra leadership camps, and earn other badges, you may end up with a class called "Leadership Studies."

Again, I recommend using the Sticky Note Strategy. For each badge your child earns in Scouts or for each project in 4-H, write the experience and course title ideas on the sticky note, e.g. animal husbandry. Put the year completed and give a grade for the experience. You could, for example, give an *A* if your child delivered two baby goats and write down the number of hours spent.

Consider possible subject areas. There are many badges to earn in Scouts and awards to win in 4-H that qualify as fine arts. Wood working, whittling, crochet, and knitting are fine arts. Use "Fine Arts" or "Crafting" as course titles.

Using the Sticky Note Strategy for Scouts and 4-H is incredibly important. Sometimes the activities go into more than one credit. You'll have multiple classes but don't double dip — make sure each topic they worked on and each activity has its own sticky note. At the end of the year, group those sticky notes together and figure out what courses they can become or be added to.

8. Speech and Debate

This is a common subject for homeschool students. You can either call a speech class "Public Speaking," or call it "Speech and Debate" if your child is involved in a speech and debate club.

You can also use speech and debate as a history or English class. Be careful about double dipping, though. Each hour can only be used one time for one class on the transcript.

Chapter 10

Finding Freedom with Homeschool Electives

There are a wide variety of electives you can choose from. One of your jobs as parents is to make sure your child isn't working too hard and that they have balance in life. If your child has many electives, you may want to explain them in a cover letter. Explain how you allowed for delight directed learning and year-round schooling. Homeschooling is an efficient form of education and that allowed plenty of time for electives. Often, they'll understand why your child earned eight or nine credits per year instead of six credits per year since you homeschool in the summer.

Celebrate your independence responsibly. Make sure you're in control of your homeschool, not delegating to a school group that approves the classes you have created for electives. Keep a firm grip on the benefits of homeschooling independently to allow your child to learn with reckless abandon. You don't need to be a certified teacher to teach your own electives. You don't need college credentials to homeschool your children.

Teachers go to teacher's college and learn how to teach groups and manage a classroom. Those skills are valuable for classroom teaching, but they're not necessary for homeschool teaching. We're only homeschooling perhaps a handful of children at a time. Don't let anyone make you feel afraid of college, scholarships, transcripts, diplomas, or career preparation. Every parent is capable of homeschooling their child successfully into adulthood.

When you embrace the freedom of homeschooling, you can find electives that can improve scholarships as colleges see that your child is genuinely interested. It can demonstrate why they selected their major, when they're already moving in that direction, as demonstrated through their electives in high school.

A kid in a public high school may have four years of auto-mechanics classes and when they apply as an auto-mechanic, the employer will look at the transcript, everything on it will make sense and it will make your child more qualified. The same is true whether your child wants to go into college or directly into a career. The person hiring them or admitting them will see their electives and will understand their interests.

Whatever classes your child has done — whether you *directed traffic* or stood back and watched it happen — I encourage you to put them on the high school transcript. All the good things your child has accomplished will be on their transcript; all their strengths will be clearly visible. Any child, regardless of abilities, will look marvelous in black and white when you include high school electives on their transcript.

Appendix

Including Bible Classes on the Transcript

Homeschoolers are often Christian families who want to give their children a Christian education. Christian high schools include faith-based classes on their transcripts and so can you! But you may wonder how to include study of your faith on your child's transcript.

I wanted to include Bible on my children's transcripts, as a full and accurate description of what they studied. Christian universities were used to seeing these classes from Christian high school applicants and public universities also saw transcripts from Christian schools. I knew that public universities love diversity and that emphasizing our Biblical worldview would bring much-desired diversity to secular campuses.

As for any class, 120 to 180 hours is one credit, and 60 to 90 hours is half a credit. If your child works for an hour per day on biblical study, then give one credit. If your child works half an hour per day, then give a half credit. If you use a curriculum that says it's a semester, then it's a half credit.

I encourage you to choose a specific class title when you can. Instead of calling the class "Bible," mention the topic covered or give a more descriptive title. First, look over the resources you are using. If you use a curriculum for a theology class, then you can call it "Bible: Theology." If you primarily study the Old Testament, you can call it "Bible: Old Testament." Consider these ideas:

- New Testament
- Old Testament

- Wisdom Literature
- Epistles of Paul
- Bible Worldview
- Biblical History
- Biblical Studies
- Philosophy
- Christian Life
- Worldviews
- Comparative Religions
- Bible as Literature

Decide whether you want Bible class to be included as an elective or as a required course. As for each core and elective class, create a course description for your child's Bible class.

Bible class can include morning devotions, scripture, church attendance, youth group, and regular faith-based non-fiction, like mine did. I didn't use a curriculum and my goal was for my children to grow up, love the Lord, and enjoy reading scripture. Our Bible class was a normal part of our lives.

Some secular colleges won't consider a Bible class part of the GPA, but some Christian colleges want to see Bible classes so they know kids are prepared. Don't worry about what the college thinks, though. Your job is to make a transcript that is honest and true. If Bible class was part of your homeschool, award the credit.

Afterword

Who is Lee Binz and What Can She Do for Me?

Number one best-selling homeschool author, Lee Binz is The HomeScholar. Her mission is "helping parents homeschool high school." Lee and her husband, Matt, homeschooled their two boys, Kevin and Alex, from elementary through high school.

Upon graduation, both boys received four-year, full tuition scholarships from their first choice university. This enables Lee to pursue her dream job — helping parents homeschool their children through high school.

On The HomeScholar website, you will find great products for creating homeschool transcripts and comprehensive records to help you amaze and impress colleges.

Find out why Andrew Pudewa, Founder of the Institute for Excellence in Writing says, "Lee Binz knows how to navigate this often confusing and frustrating labyrinth better than anyone."

You can find Lee online at:

HomeHighSchoolHelp.com

If this book has been helpful, could you please take a minute to write us a quick review on Amazon? Thank you!

Testimonials

Your Advice Was Personalized Just for Me!

I wanted to reach out and thank you for today's free workshop. I am in the final crunch of compiling my daughter's comprehensive record and transcript as we are on the cusp of submitting applications. I decided to join the workshop to remind myself that our homeschool is a real learning experience that deserves documentation and to encourage myself to the end of the application process by joining other families who are passionate about this topic.

I felt motivated when you asked me to commit to setting a time on my calendar to finish the course descriptions and you gave me permission to put all the other basic household tasks on hold so that the comprehensive record has priority. Your clarity on where and how to derive course descriptions drove into me that I can complete this work and do it well. Finally, just putting your voice to the words I have read on your website and from your book made me feel that your advice was personalized just for me.

~Amanda in New Jersey

Best Transcript Ever!

I just wanted to share some encouraging news that we have so far on Rio.

He has been accepted at Corban, Whitworth, Northwest, SPU, and just finished applying for UW. Basically, all the private colleges he has applied for with the highest scholarships available without the special competition, he has been invited to the honors programs and the full-tuition competitions (haven't heard back from George Fox yet). So praise the Lord for a good start

Here's what I really want to tell you - when Rio went to interview for SPU, the admission counselor praised the Comprehensive Record Rio submitted, saying he had never seen anything like that before. Best transcript ever for it was clear, organized and easy to navigate. Yay! thank you so much for all your help, Lee!

~Sanea in Washington

For more information about my **Comprehensive Record Solution**, go to:

www.ComprehensiveRecordSolution.com

Also From The HomeScholar...

- The HomeScholar Guide to College Admission and Scholarships: Homeschool Secrets to Getting Ready, Getting in and Getting Paid (Book and Kindle Book)

- Setting the Records Straight — How to Craft Homeschool Transcripts and Course Descriptions for College Admission and Scholarships (Book and Kindle Book)

- TechnoLogic: How to Set Logical Technology Boundaries and Stop the Zombie Apocalypse

- Finding the Faith to Homeschool High School

- Parent Training A la Carte (Online Training)
- Total Transcript Solution (Online Training, Tools and Templates)
- Comprehensive Record Solution (Online Training, Tools and Templates)
- High School Solution (Online Training, Tools, Templates, and Support)
- College Launch Solution (Online Training, Tools, Templates, and Support)
- Gold Care Club (Comprehensive Online Support and Training)
- Silver Training Club (Online Training)

The HomeScholar Coffee Break Books Released or Coming Soon on Kindle and Paperback:

- Delight Directed Learning: Guiding Your Homeschooler Toward Passionate Learning
- Creating Transcripts for Your Unique Child: Help Your Homeschool Graduate Stand Out from the Crowd
- Beyond Academics: Preparation for College and for Life
- Planning High School Courses: Charting the Course Toward High School Graduation
- Graduate Your Homeschooler in Style: Make Your Homeschool Graduation Memorable
- Keys to High School Success: Get Your Homeschool High School Started Right!

- Getting the Most Out of Your Homeschool This Summer: Learning Just for the Fun of it!

- Finding a College: A Homeschooler's Guide to Finding a Perfect Fit

- College Scholarships for High School Credit: Learn and Earn with This Two-for-One Strategy!

- College Admission Policies Demystified: Understanding Homeschool Requirements for Getting In

- A Higher Calling: Homeschooling High School for Harried Husbands (by Matt Binz, Mr. HomeScholar)

- Gifted Education Strategies for Every Child: Homeschool Secrets for Success

- College Application Essays: A Primer for Parents

- Creating Homeschool Balance: Find Harmony Between Type A and Type Zzz...

- Homeschooling the Holidays: Sanity Saving Strategies and Gift Giving Ideas

- Your Goals this Year: A Year by Year Guide to Homeschooling High School

- Making the Grades: A Grouch-Free Guide to Homeschool Grading

- High School Testing: Knowledge That Saves Money

- Getting the BIG Scholarships: Learn Expert Secrets for Winning College Cash!

- Easy English for Simple Homeschooling: How to Teach, Assess and Document High School English

- Scheduling — The Secret to Homeschool Sanity: Plan You Way Back to Mental Health

- Junior Year is the Key to High School Success: How to Unlock the Gate to Graduation and Beyond

- Upper Echelon Education: How to Gain Admission to Elite Universities

- How to Homeschool College: Save Time, Reduce Stress and Eliminate Debt

- Homeschool Curriculum That's Effective and Fun: Avoid the Crummy Curriculum Hall of Shame!

- Comprehensive Homeschool Records: Put Your Best Foot Forward to Win College Admission and Scholarships

- Options After High School: Steps to Success for College or Career

- How to Homeschool 9th and 10th Grades: Simple Steps for Starting Strong!

- Senior Year Step-by-Step: Simple Instructions for Busy Homeschool Parents

- How to Homeschool Independently: Do-it-Yourself Secrets to Rekindle the Love of Learning

- High School Math the Easy Way: Simple Strategies for Homeschool Parents in Over Their Heads

- Homeschooling Middle School with Powerful Purpose: How to Successfully Navigate 6th through 8th Grades

- Simple Science for Homeschooling High School: Because Teaching Science isn't Rocket Science!

- How to Be Your Child's Best College Coach: Launch: Strategies for

Success Using Teens You'll Find Lying Around the House

- Teen Tips for College and Career Success: Learn Why 10 C's are Better Than All A's or APs
- How to Motivate Homeschool Teens: Strategies for Inspiring Slug-Slow Students

Would you like to be notified when we offer the next *Coffee Break Books* FREE during our Kindle promotion days? If so, leave your name and email below and we will send you a reminder.

HomeHighSchoolHelp.com/freekindlebook

Visit my Amazon Author Page!
amazon.com/author/leebinz

Made in the USA
Las Vegas, NV
23 May 2023